40 CHARACTERISTIC ETUDES FOR FRENCH HORN

by H. KLING
Edited and Revised by LORENZO SANSONE

Allegro vivace.

Nº 1.

2

Souvenir d' Auber. (*Erinnerung an Auber.*)
Moderato.

Nº 2.

Souvenir de Mozart. (*Erinnerung an Mozart.*)
Allegro moderato.

Nº 3.

4

Souvenir de Rossini. (*Erinnerung an Rossini.*)
Allegro moderato.

Nᵒ.4.

Allegro.

Nᵒ5.

7

6

ROMANZE.
Andante con moto.

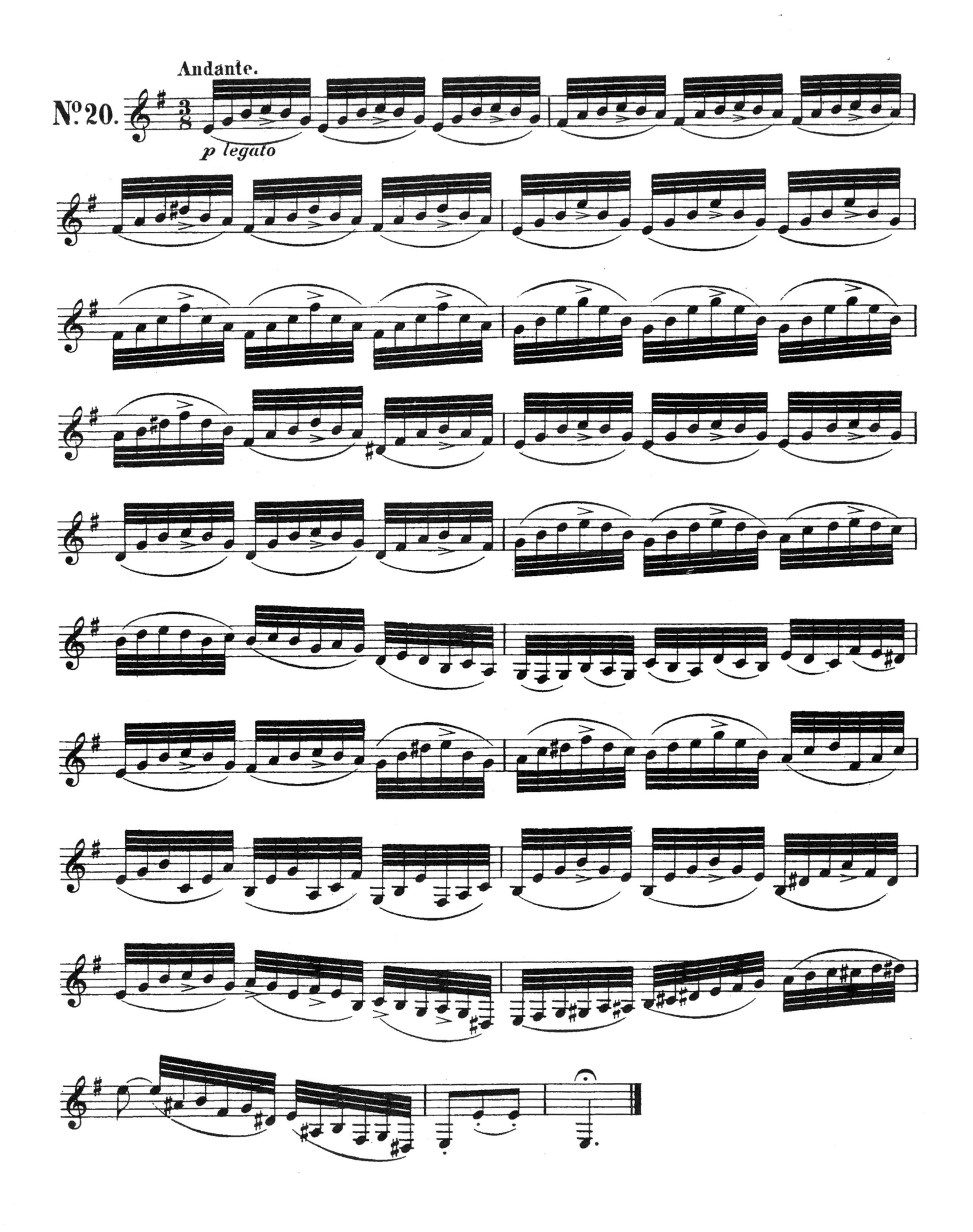

ROMANZE.
Tempo moderato.

Nº 28.

24

Souvenir d' Haydn. (*Erinnerung an Haydn.*)
Andante.

Nº 29.

Souvenir de Mozart. (*Erinnerung an Mozart.*)
Allegro moderato.

Nº 30.

30

Allegro scherzando.

N° 39.

Tempo di Valse.

№ 40.